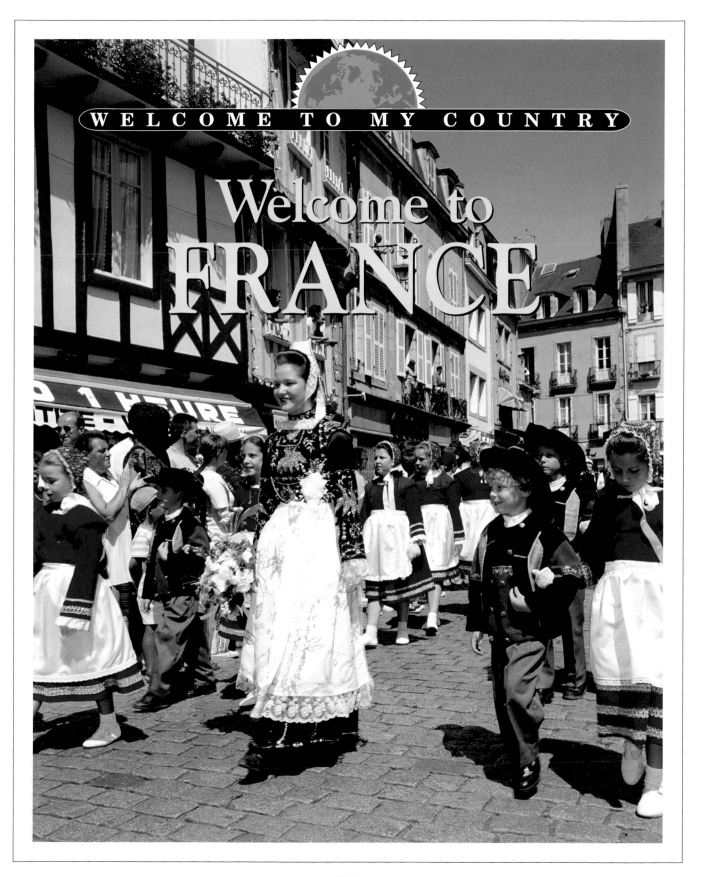

Welcome to
FRANCE

FRANKLIN WATTS
LONDON • SYDNEY

This edition first published in 2006 by
Franklin Watts
338 Euston Road
London NW1 3BH

This edition is published for sale only in the United Kingdom and Eire.

© Marshall Cavendish International (Asia) Pte Ltd 2006
Originated and designed by Times Editions–Marshall Cavendish
An imprint of Marshall Cavendish International (Asia) Pte Ltd
1 New Industrial Road, Singapore 536196

Written by: Fiona Conboy & Roseline NgCheong-Lum
Designer: Benson Tan
Picture researchers: Thomas Khoo & Joshua Ang

A CIP catalogue record for this book
is available from the British Library.

ISBN-10: 0 7496 7022 3
ISBN-13: 978 0 7496 7022 1

Printed in Malaysia

Franklin Watts is a division of Hachette Children's Books.

Contents

Words that appear in the glossary are printed in **bold** the first time they occur in the text.

Welcome to France!

The largest nation in Western Europe, France has been a leader in the arts for many centuries. It is also a country of contrasts. Its culture combines traditional values and modern style. Let's explore the land of delicious cuisine and elegant fashions and learn more about the French!

Opposite: Many quaint villages fill the French countryside.

Below: French children go to primary school at the age of six.

The Flag of France

The French flag is made up of blue, red and white panels. It is called the Tricolour. Blue and red are the colours of France's capital city, Paris. White was the colour of the kings of France between 1638 and 1790.

The Land

France covers an area of 547,030 square kilometres in Europe. Various territories in the Mediterranean Sea, the Caribbean Sea, the Pacific Ocean,

the Indian Ocean, the Atlantic Ocean and Antarctica also belong to France.

The Massif Central, a large, granite **plateau**, makes up one-sixth of the country. The plateau is lined with deep gorges and is dotted with extinct volcanoes, crater lakes and hot

Above: The French Alps stretch along the border with Switzerland and Italy in southeastern France. Mont Blanc, in the French Alps, is the highest peak in France at 4,805 metres.

mineral springs, including the health spa of Vichy.

Mountainous regions form France's borders with Italy in the southeast and Spain in the south. One of these, the French Alps, boasts many popular ski

resorts. The highest peaks there are called the Massif du Mont Blanc.

France is famous for its rivers, which include the Seine, the Rhône and the Rhine. For centuries, the French crossed the country by boat on these rivers.

Above: In the days before cars, trains and planes, rivers and canals formed an important communications network for the different regions in France.

Climate

The French climate varies greatly from region to region. The Riviera is warm, while the mountain areas are colder. In the northwest, the Atlantic Ocean brings wet weather.

Left: In Alsace, snow covers the mountain slopes during the cold winter months.

Plants and Animals

Forests cover about one quarter of France. Wild animals, such as snakes, brown bears, wolves and deer, live in the forests and national parks, while antelope roam the mountains.

Left: Storks migrate to France from Africa during the summer months. They build their nests in treetops and on the roofs of tall buildings.

The coastal areas are home to a variety of birds and sea creatures. Efforts by the National Forestry Office have increased the amount of forested areas since 1945.

History

Gaul and the Roman Empire

The **Celts** (KELTS) were the first to invade France, which was earlier known as Gaul. In 52 BCE, Roman emperor Julius Caesar defeated the Gaul chief Vercingetorix. For the next 500 years, the Romans ruled Gaul. In the fifth century, Germanic tribes invaded and conquered the Romans.

Below: The defeated Celtic leader Vercingetorix lays down his arms before Roman emperor Julius Caesar.

The Middle Ages

During a period known as the **Middle Ages**, France was the most powerful kingdom in Western Europe. In 1337, France and England fought each other in the Hundred Years' War. With the help of a young girl, Joan of Arc, the French army saved France from English occupation.

Renaissance and Reformation

The **Renaissance** came to France from Italy in the fifteenth century. It was a time of scholarly learning in Europe.

In the sixteenth century, the **Reformation** created the Protestant Church in France. Catholics and Protestants fought each other for many years.

During the seventeenth century, Louis XIV ruled France. Said to be one of the greatest kings of France, he encouraged the French to explore the land now known as North America.

Above: Louis XIV, also known as the Sun King, was said to glow with a glorious light. Classical art and literature flourished during his reign.

Above: The English were about to conquer France when Joan of Arc led French troops to victory at Orleans in 1429. She was named a saint in 1920, almost 500 years after her death.

The French Revolution

In 1789, conflicts between French commoners and the nobility led to the French Revolution. It lasted 10 years. In 1792, the **monarchy** was abolished, and King Louis XVI and his wife, Marie Antoinette, were found guilty of **treason**. They were executed.

During the revolution, an officer named Napoleon Bonaparte rose to

Above: On 14 July 1789, a mob of angry peasants stormed the Bastille, a prison in Paris. Throughout the land, castles were invaded and destroyed by commoners who were unhappy with the privileges bestowed on the French **aristocracy**.

power. In 1799, he formed a new government. France went to war against the rest of Europe. Napoleon became emperor but was eventually defeated by other European armies.

By the early 1900s, France and Britain had become **allies**. Russia and Britain defended France from the Germans during World War I (1914–1918). Almost two million French soldiers died during the war. The United States, which entered the war in 1917, helped France drive the Germans out and win back conquered territories.

Left: The Arc de Triomphe in Paris was built to celebrate the victories of Napoleon. After each of the world wars, troops marched through the Arc in triumph. A national remembrance service is held there each year to honour those who lost their lives in battle.

World War II

In 1939, Germany invaded Poland, and Britain and France declared war against the Germans. The Germans invaded Paris in 1940 and established a government in the south. During World War II, General Charles de Gaulle led a French rebel group, the Resistance, against the Germans. In 1944, British, American and Canadian soldiers landed in France and freed it from German occupation. World War II formally ended in 1945.

Above: Charles de Gaulle's goal after World War II was to make France the leader of Europe.

After the War

In 1959, Charles de Gaulle became president of France. However, some of the French were dissatisfied with his government. In the 1960s, university students organised a series of **demonstrations** against the way the country was run. The French government survived by making widespread **reforms.** Today, France holds a strong position in world affairs.

Charlemagne (742–814)

Charlemagne, or Charles the Great, ruled France from 768 to 814. In 800, he was crowned emperor of a vast region that included most of Western Europe.

Charlemagne

Marie Antoinette (1755–1793)

Marie Antoinette was not a popular queen – particularly with the poorer people of France. When she heard that the peasants did not have any bread, she told them to eat cake instead!

Marie Antoinette

Napoleon Bonaparte (1769–1821)

Napoleon led France in wars against the rest of Western Europe in the late 1700s and early 1800s. He was defeated in 1815. He developed the Napoleonic Code for France, a series of laws that forms the basis of French law today.

Napoleon Bonaparte

Government and the Economy

France is a **republic** led by a **democratically** elected president. The president makes important decisions about national and foreign affairs. He or she also appoints the prime minister, who looks after the day-to-day running of the country.

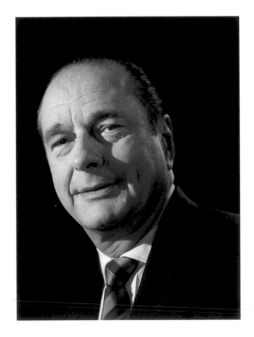 

Jacques Chirac (*far left*) has been president of France since 1995. Lionel Jospin (*left*) was Chirac's prime minister from 1997 to 2002.

France's 22 regions are divided into 96 departments, each run by a local council and an official from the main government.

Elections

Two houses – the National Assembly and the Senate – make up the French parliament. Every French citizen over the age of 18 has the right to vote for a president and members of parliament. Citizens also vote for their local councils.

National Service

Until 2001, all French males between the ages of 18 and 35 were required to serve in the army, navy or air force for one year.

Agriculture

France has one of the world's strongest economies. Agriculture is an important sector. France produces crops, such as wheat, corn, sugar beet and grapes.

France is well-known for its fine wines as well as delicious dairy products, such as milk, cheese and cream. French beef and veal are exported to other European countries. In the northern part of France, the fishing industry thrives.

Below: Fishermen in Brittany bring ashore many types of fresh seafood.

Left: The fastest passenger plane in the world was the Concorde, made by Air France and British Airways. It reached speeds of 2,140 kilometres per hour. After 27 years, the Concorde was withdrawn from service in 2003.

An Economic Leader

France has become a world leader in technology. Besides cars, satellites and telecommunications equipment, France manufactures advanced civilian and military aircraft and high-speed trains, such as the TGV.

France was one of the founding members of the European Union (EU), a group of European countries with strong economic ties and a common currency. France trades with other EU countries, as well as with the United States, Japan and Russia.

Below: A grape picker examines a bunch of grapes at a vineyard on the outskirts of Nice, in the southeast of France.

19

People and Lifestyle

More than 60 million people live in France. Their appearance reflects the many groups – Alpine, Nordic and Mediterranean – from which they descend. Northerners tend to be blonde with blue eyes, whereas southerners may be darker and smaller. During the last hundred years, **immigrants** have arrived from many countries, including Italy, Poland and North Africa.

Above: A large number of North African immigrants live in France.

Social Classes

There is a strong social structure in France. Many people in the upper class, or aristocracy, live in the grand homes of their ancestors. However, they no longer have the power they once held. The middle class, or *bourgeoisie* (boor-zhwah-ZEE), is the largest and most influential group. Most professionals belong to this group. Farmers and manual workers form the working class. The distinction between the middle and working classes is diminishing.

Below: Friends and family share in the fun during a big Bastille Day picnic. The French love spending leisure time together.

Rural Life

Life in the French countryside is quiet. After World War II, many villagers moved to towns and cities to look for jobs. As a result, many rural houses are now used as holiday homes. For the people who still live in the countryside, social and leisure activities usually centre on the village square.

Above: Farmers use tractors to work their fields.

City Life

Approximately one-sixth of France's population – about 10.5 million people – live in Paris. Other major cities are Lyon, Marseille, Bordeaux

and Lille. Grand old buildings, once the homes of the aristocracy, are found in most city centres. Today, they function as offices or small apartments but retain their elegance and charm. Homes in the city centre are expensive, so most people live in the **suburbs**. French families, especially those in the cities, tend to be small.

Above: The streets of Paris always bustle with shoppers and tourists.

Women

In the late nineteenth century, French women began the fight for women's rights in their country. In 1945, women were given the right to vote. Today, they enjoy legal equality with men. One of the most famous French women is Marie Curie. Her scientific work on radioactivity paved the way for cancer treatment. France's first female prime minister was Edith Cresson, elected in 1991.

Above: Scientists Marie and Pierre Curie studied radioactivity. In 1906, Marie Curie became the first woman to be appointed professor at the Sorbonne University in Paris.

Left: More and more women in France work in jobs outside the home, but their salaries are still lower than men's.

Education

The **literacy rate** in France is high – 99.2 per cent of adults can read and write. Schooling is free and required for children between the ages of six and sixteen. Primary school lasts for six years and is followed by four years of secondary school. Three years of *lycée* (li-SAY), or high school, follow secondary school, after which the top students attend a university.

Above: In addition to their regular school lessons, young French students sometimes take classes in music, dance and art.

Christianity

Until the French Revolution of 1789–1799, the official religion of France was Roman Catholicism. After the Revolution, France was declared simply "Christian". Today, more than 80 per cent of the population is Christian – mainly Roman Catholic. However, less than 10 per cent of this number attend church regularly.

Above: The Madeleine Roman Catholic church in Paris was consecrated in 1842. Catholicism is a little less **dominant** in France since the Revolution. Until then, most children were named after Catholic saints.

Islam

After Christianity, Islam is the second largest religion in France. Many Muslims originally came from North Africa. Today, Muslims make up about 7 to 10 per cent of the population.

Judaism

One per cent of the population is Jewish. Today, there are more Jews in France than in any other country in Western Europe.

Below: This part of Paris is home mainly to Jewish people.

Language

The French language is derived from Latin. Romans brought it to Gaul in 52 BCE. Before this, the Gauls spoke Celtic languages. Between the ninth and fourteenth centuries, two **dialects** were spoken – *langue d'oc* (LAHNG dohk) in the north, and *langue d'oïl* (LAHNG doy) in the south. The northern dialect was adopted as the common language. Today, more than 250 million people in the world speak French.

Left: French writers Paule Constant (*left*) and Dominique Bona (*right*) have won major awards for their novels.

Far left: Victor Hugo (1802–1855) wrote *Les Miserables*, a novel based on the French Revolution.

Left: Aurore Dudevant (1804–1876) wrote novels and short stories under the pen name "George Sand".

Literature

France has produced some of the greatest writers of all time. Their works are studied throughout the world.

Classical plays by Pierre Corneille, Jean Racine and Jean-Baptiste Molière charmed King Louis XIV and his court.

During the nineteenth century, Victor Hugo wrote *The Hunchback of Notre Dame,* and Alexandre Dumas penned *The Three Musketeers*. Other French literary greats include Marcel Proust, Jean Paul Sartre, Albert Camus, Simone de Beauvoir and Hélène Cixous.

Arts

Painting

Over 15,000 years ago, prehistoric artists created the world's first paintings in caves in France.

In the nineteenth century, artists of the impressionist movement used colour and light to portray people and

landscapes as they looked at particular times of the day. Claude Monet's painting, *Impression: Sunrise*, gave this artistic style its name. Another famous impressionist painter is Édouard Manet.

Top: *Argentueil,* 1874, by painter Édouard Manet.

Above: Visitors to the Louvre, an art museum in Paris, enter through this glass pyramid.

Film

Drawing on American Thomas Edison's inventions, Frenchmen Louis and Auguste Lumière invented the film projector in the nineteenth century.

Today, France produces hundreds of films every year. French films are well-known for their wit and their reflections on human nature.

Left: The best new films of the year are launched at the Cannes Film Festival in France. The festival includes new films from all around the world.

Architecture

The changing tastes of the French are reflected in the country's many architectural styles. The dramatic **Gothic** style developed between the twelfth and fifteenth centuries. The Renaissance followed, and fine castles and churches appeared across France.

The spectacular Palace of Versailles in Paris was built during the reign of King Louis XIV. France's most famous structure, the Eiffel Tower, was built for an exhibition in 1889.

Above: Notre Dame Cathedral is a magnificent example of Gothic architecture. It features stained-glass windows and tall, elaborate spires.

Lace-Making

Brittany, in northwestern France, is one of the few regions where lace-making still thrives. Lace-making and other traditional crafts are practised in many French towns and villages.

Leisure

The Great Outdoors

The French love to spend their leisure time outdoors. The changing landscape provides great spots for a variety of activities, including hiking, climbing, cycling, horseriding and skiing.

Many French city dwellers have second homes in the countryside. They travel there on weekends and for long vacations to relax and escape city life.

Above: Cyclists ride through the countryside of the Dauphiné region of France during an annual bicycle race.

Boules

Boules (BOOL) is a popular game in southern France. It is played with small, metal balls. Each player rolls a ball towards a smaller one, the *cochonnet* (ko-cho-NAY). The player whose ball lands closest to the cochonnet wins the game.

Left: A man takes aim before rolling one of the metal balls in a game of boules in Provence.

Sport

Football is probably the most popular sport in France. In 1998, France hosted and won the World Cup, beating the favourite, Brazil, in the final.

Individual sports, such as skiing, cycling and horseriding, are popular, too. The Alps provide some of the best ski slopes in the world. The Tour de France, the biggest cycling event of the year, covers between 3,000 and 4,000 kilometres.

Above: The French Alps are popular with skiers.

Below: The best cyclists in the world take part in the Tour de France every year.

Festivals

Many festivals take place throughout the year in France. The biggest are the Christian celebrations of Christmas and Easter. On 6 January, or Twelfth Night, children celebrate Epiphany. A special pastry containing a surprise is served. The child who receives the surprise is made king or queen for the day. Just before Lent (the forty-day period of fasting before Easter), Carnival is celebrated.

Below: Carnival is a festival of parades, colour and costumes. It is the time of celebration before Lent.

Bastille Day

Bastille Day falls on 14 July. It marks the beginning of the French Revolution and is celebrated as France's national day. The Tricolour flag flies in every city and town, and fireworks light up the night skies.

Above: A dramatic fireworks display illuminates the Eiffel Tower in Paris on Bastille Day.

Festival de Cournouaille

Every year in July, the streets of Brittany are filled with Celtic culture. There are puppet shows, lace-making demonstrations, wrestling matches and dancing. This is the Festival de Cournouaille, when **Bretons** celebrate their Celtic roots.

Avignon Festival

The Avignon Festival, France's largest arts festival, takes place during July and August. During the event, the town of Avignon comes alive with music and dancing. The festival has been held every year since it was founded by

well-known French actors Gérard Philipe and Jean Vilar in 1947.

Vendanges

Each September, grape harvest festivals, called *vendanges* (von-DAHNGES), celebrate the year's new wines. Many people enjoy wine tasting and folk dancing. The most important vendanges take place in Burgundy.

Above: The people of Saint-Tropez, a town on France's Mediterranean coast, celebrate the Bravades festival in May in honour of their patron saint and their military past.

Food

France is famous for its delicious cuisine, and French food is served in restaurants all over the world. Each region in France has a special dish. *Bouillabaisse* (boo-yah-BES) is a rich seafood stew from the Mediterranean

coast. Ratatouille, from Provence, is a vegetable dish made with herbs and olive oil. Along the Atlantic coast, fresh oysters, served raw or cooked, are a favourite.

Above: Bread is so important to the French that the law requires each town or village to have a bakery selling fresh bread every day.

Family Meals

A favourite breakfast in France is a *croissant* (CWAH-son) – a rich, flaky pastry – served with a large cup of coffee or hot chocolate.

Sunday lunch is the biggest meal of the week. The entire family gathers at

home for a three-course meal of soup, roast meat and a rich dessert. During the week, most people have a light lunch. The main meal of the day is dinner in the evening.

Above: The French love to sit in outdoor cafés and enjoy a snack or a cup of coffee in the fresh air.

FRANCE

A B C D

1 2 3 4 5

ENGLAND

NORTH
SEA

NETHERLANDS

BELGIUM

LUXEMBOURG

Lille

NORD-PAS-DE-
CALAIS

UPPER
NORMANDY

PICARDIE

LORRAINE

English Channel

LOWER
NORMANDY

Seine

Versailles ■ PARIS
ÎLE-DE-
FRANCE

CHAMPAGNE-
ARDENNE

Domrémy

Rhine

BRITTANY
(BRETAGNE)

PAYS DE
LA LOIRE

Orléans

CENTRE

Dijon

FRANCHE-
COMTÉ

ATLANTIC
OCEAN

Loire

BURGUNDY
(BOURGOGNE)

Vichy

POITOU-
CHARENTES

LIMOUSIN

Lyon

Mont Blanc
(4,805 m)

Bay of
Biscay

AUVERGNE

Massif

RHÔNE-
ALPES

A
L
P
E
S

Bordeaux
AQUITAINE

Central

Rhône

PROVENCE-ALPES-
CÔTE-D'AZUR

MIDI-PYRÉNÉES

Avignon

Cannes

Marseille

Lourdes

P Y R E N E E S

LANGUEDOC-
ROUSSILLON

French Riviera

	International Boundary
	State Boundary
■	Capital
●	City
〜	River
▲	Mountain

ANDORRA

SPAIN

MEDITERRANEAN
SEA

E

N

GERMANY

ALSACE

SWITZERLAND

ITALY

MONACO

CORSICA
(France)

Alps D4
Alsace E2
Andorra C5
Aquitaine B4
Atlantic Ocean A3
Auvergne C3–C4
Avignon D4

Bay of Biscay A4
Belgium D1
Bordeaux B4
Brittany A2–B2
Burgundy C3–D3

Cannes D4
Centre C2–C3
Champagne-Ardenne
    C2–D2
Corsica E5

Dijon D3
Domrémy D2

England B1
English Channel A2

Franche-Comté D3
French Riviera D5

Germany E1

Île-de-France C2
Italy E4

Languedoc-
    Roussillon C5
Lille C1
Limousin C3
Loire River B3
Lorraine D2
Lourdes B5
Lower Normandy B2
Luxembourg D1–D2
Lyon D3

Marseille D5
Massif Central C4
Mediterranean
    Sea D5

Above: A fountain at the Palace of Versailles.

Midi-Pyrénées
    B5–C5
Monaco E4
Mont Blanc D3

Netherlands D1
Nord-Pas-de-Calais
    C1
North Sea C1

Orléans C2

Paris C2
Pays de la Loire
    B2–B3
Picardie C2
Poitou-Charentes B3

Provence-Alpes-
    Côtes D'Azur D4
Pyrénées B5

Rhine River E2
Rhône-Alpes D3–D4
Rhône River D4

Seine River C2
Spain A5–C5
Switzerland E3

Upper Normandy
    B2–C2

Versailles C2
Vichy C3

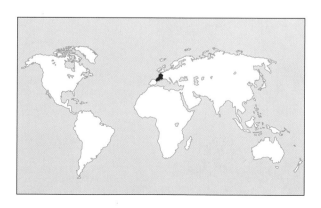

Quick Facts

Official Name   The French Republic

Capital   Paris

Official Language   French

Population   60,876,136 (July 2006 estimate)

Land Area   547,030 square kilometres

Regions   Alsace, Aquitaine, Auvergne, Brittany, Burgundy, Centre, Champagne-Ardenne, Corsica, Franche-Comté, Île-de-France, Languedoc-Roussillon, Limousin, Lorraine, Lower Normandy, Midi-Pyrénées, Nord-Pas-de-Calais, Pays de la Loire, Picardie, Poitou-Charentes, Provence-Alpes-Côte d'Azur, Rhône-Alpes, Upper Normandy, overseas departments and territories

Highest Point   Mont Blanc (4,805 metres)

Longest River   Loire River (1,020 kilometres)

Main Religion   Roman Catholicism

National Anthem   "La Marseillaise"

Currency   Euro

Opposite: Ornate windows and walls surround the court of this building in Lille.

Glossary

allies: nations that provide military and/or economic support for each other.

aristocracy: members of the upper class, who have usually descended from nobility.

Breton: from Brittany; someone who lives in Brittany.

Celts (KELTS): a group of people who originated in the British Isles.

cuisine (KWEE-zeen)**:** food.

democratically: according to the principles of a system of government that is for the people and by the people.

demonstrations: public displays of the attitudes of certain groups towards certain political or social issues.

dialects: regional varieties of a particular language.

dominant: ruling or controlling.

Gothic: a style of architecture popular in Europe from the twelfth to the sixteenth centuries.

immigrants: people who move to a country that is different from the one in which they were born.

integrated: blended into.

literacy rate: the percentage of people who can read and write.

lycée (li-SAY)**:** high school.

Middle Ages: the period in European history from about 500 to 1500 CE.

monarchy: a country or government ruled by a king or queen.

plateau: a large area of flat land that is higher than the surrounding areas.

Reformation: the sixteenth-century movement in Europe that split the Catholic Church into the Catholic and Protestant churches.

reforms: changes that improve a particular system.

Renaissance: the movement in Europe between the fifteenth and seventeenth centuries that revived interest in literature and the arts and produced a creative flowering.

republic: a country in which supreme power rests with the people, who elect representatives to govern.

suburbs: residential districts that are outside the city centre.

treason: the act of betraying a ruler, government or country.

More Books to Read

The Magical Garden of Claude Monet. Lawrence Anholt (Francis Lincoln)

Degas and the Little Dancer. Lawrence Anholt (Francis Lincoln)

Joan of Arc of Domremy. Michael Morpurgo (Hodder Children's Books)

France. Country File series. C Tichmarsh (Franklin Watts)

France. Country Insights series. Teresa Fisher (Hodder Wayland)

France. Changing Face of series. Virginia Chandler (Hodder Wayland)

Take your camera to France. Ted Park (Raintree)

Websites

www.culture.fr/culture/arcnat/lascaux/en

www.teacher.scholastic.com/activities/globaltrek/destinations/France.htm

Due to the dynamic nature of the Internet, some websites stay current longer than others. To find additional websites about France, use a reliable search engine and enter one or more of the following keywords. Keywords: *Charlemagne, Jacques Chirac, French Revolution, impressionist painters, Joan of Arc, Louis XIV, Louvre, Paris.*

Note to parents and teachers

Every effort has been made by the Publishers to ensure that these websites are suitable for children, that they are of the highest educational value, and that they contain no inappropriate or offensive material. However, because of the nature of the Internet, it is impossible to guarantee that the contents of these sites will not be altered. We strongly advise that Internet access is supervised by a responsible adult.

Index